GREENPORT THROUGH TIME

The Story of a Historic Seaport Village

RICHARD PANCHYK

AMERICA THROUGH TIME®
ADDING COLOR TO AMERICAN HISTORY

Acknowledgments

Thanks as always to Alan Sutton and Kena Longabaugh for their support and assistance. Special thanks to one of my amazing friends Richard Kind for writing the Afterword. Thanks to Terry Keefe at the Silver Sands for his help. And special thanks to Lizz and Matt.

Photo Credits

Library of Congress: pages 11, 13 (top), 19 (bottom), 20 (bottom), 27 (top), 34, 35, 36, 67
National Archives: pages 21, 22 (top), 85 (top).
All other images courtesy of the author.

America Through Time is an imprint of Fonthill Media LLC
www.through-time.com
office@through-time.com

Published by Arcadia Publishing by arrangement with Fonthill Media LLC
For all general information, please contact Arcadia Publishing:
Telephone: 843-853-2070
Fax: 843-853-0044
E-mail: sales@arcadiapublishing.com
For customer service and orders:
Toll-Free 1-888-313-2665

www.arcadiapublishing.com

First published 2022

ISBN 978-1-63499-409-5

Typeset in Mrs Eaves XL Serif Narrow
Printed and bound in England

INTRODUCTION

Steeped in a rich maritime history dating back to the whaling era, today's Greenport is a lively, colorful village that celebrates its seafaring heritage while also embracing its newer status as a fun and trendy North Fork getaway destination. Walking along its streets, you get the sense of a place that has preserved its past without sacrificing the need for growth and change. In doing so, Greenport has become a very special and unique locale that is both quaint and modern, sweetly tranquil and yet pulsating with vibrant energy at the same time.

Originally known as Stirling (among other names), the Greenport area was first settled in the mid-seventeenth century by colonists who came to eastern Long Island from Connecticut. Greenport existed as a settlement of only a few homes until the early nineteenth century. Main Street was laid out in 1827 and the first store was opened in 1828. By the 1830s, whaling had taken hold in Greenport (as it had in other eastern Long Island and New England locations) and remained an important part of Greenport life through the mid nineteenth-century. As of 1834, there were two whaling ships based out of Greenport; in 1841 there were five whaling ships, and in 1844 there were seven. The total cost of a three-year voyage could run up to an astounding $60,000 for supplies and ship combined—but with a successful whaling trip that money would be recouped and then some. The principal provisions required for the long journey included beef and pork, bread, molasses, peas, beans, corn, potatoes, dried apples, coffee, tea, chocolate, and butter.

An article in *The Sailor's Magazine* told of an 1844 religious meeting on board a whaling ship that was about to depart (with more spectators on the wharves and other nearby ships). Greenport's Presbyterian and Methodist ministers gave sermons along with "Rev. Prof. Carry" from New York City, and there was also singing, reading of Scriptures, and prayers offered for the departing sailors; according to a witness, "the whole scene was, in itself, deeply impressive."

By 1846, there were about 100 homes and 700 residents in Greenport, thanks in large part to whaling. The industry continued to grow and by 1854, there were ten whaling ships based in Greenport. That number went up to eleven in 1856, the year of Claudio's Restaurant founder Manuel Claudio's first arrival in Greenport aboard the whaling bark *Neve*. The whaling ship numbers declined quickly to nine in 1857, seven in 1858, four in 1859, two in 1860, and none in the years after that. Compare this to Sag Harbor, which had twenty whaling ships based there in 1859, a number that declined but was still eight whaling ships by 1866.

Besides whaling, commercial fishing and oystering also represented a major portion of the local economy and continued to be a vital component of Greenport's existence long after the whaling industry subsided. Menhaden were one type of fish that was sought after. These small one-pound fish are used for bait, animal feed, and fertilizer. In 1850, D. D. Wells built the first menhaden oil factory on the Atlantic coast in Greenport. The oil could be used in painting and tanning, and the refuse that was left after the oil was expressed was dried and pulverized and used as fertilizer. In 1877, the Sterling Company in Greenport, using nine ships and employing twenty-seven men and eight boys, brought in over 14 million menhaden. The average yield for oil was about 4½ gallons of oil per thousand fish. In 1880, the Greenport yield was 3 million pounds of fish, 20,000 pounds of eels, eighty barrels of lobsters, seventy-five barrels of crabs, 10,000 pounds of scallops, and 1,400 bushels of clams; sixty-four people (two men, fourteen women, forty children) were dedicated to the catching and processing of Greenport scallops alone. According to a 1925 book about Long Island, "the water front of Greenport is alive with fishing boats, big power boats, filled with live cod, furnishing a staple food to the village at a moderate price."

During the late nineteenth century, oystering became serious business in Greenport. By 1904, about 350,000 bushels of seed oysters were being planted annually near Greenport. Empty oyster (and other shells) could be salvaged and used as beds upon which the seed oysters could grow. In 1887, 130,000 bushels of empty shells were sold to oyster growers for $5,200. As of 1921, there were four oyster houses in Greenport. Oystering continued to be an important part of Greenport's economy. A 1954 feature article in *Boys' Life* magazine took a firsthand look at the lives of Greenport's oystermen. As of 1934, seventy-five commercial fishing and oyster boats, ranging in length from 30-100 feet, used Greenport Harbor as their home port. Today, oysters continue to be harvested in Greenport, notably at Pipe's Cove and Widow's Hole, two locations just east of the Silver Sands Motel.

With all these various boats calling Greenport their home, it is natural that boat repair and maintenance would become an important sub-industry. As of 1934, Preston's, Bishop's, and Ketcham's were three boat repair shops that were located along Sterling Basin.

Shipbuilding has been another of Greenport's biggest industries. As of 1933, there were six wharves, six large piers, and twelve small piers with a total linear wharfage of 9,000 feet. During peace time, Greenport shipbuilders focused on yachts and commercial boats. During World War I, there was much war-related shipbuilding activity. In fact, in 1917, before the United States entered the war, the Greenport Basin and Construction company built numerous high speed power boats (submarine chasers) for the Russian government, and also built boats for the United States Navy. In 1938, airplane rescue boats were built in Greenport for the U.S Army Air Corps, and soon after that the Greenport Basin and Construction Company was awarded a contract for eight Navy minesweepers, which were completed in 290 days total; its success resulted in another contract, for twelve minesweepers.

A regular ferry between Greenport and Shelter Island had been operating since the early nineteenth century. In 1837, the New York State legislature passed an act to incorporate the Green-port and Shelter Island ferry company, which was to "keep and maintain one good ferry-boat, to be propelled with sufficient horse or steam power, and capable of carrying two wagons and four horses, and shall also keep two good row boats."

In about 1840, Elisha Griffing Beebe made trips in a small sailboat. An official ferry charter was issued to one Jonathan Preston in 1859, and as of 1865, the ferry service's assets consisted of two sailboats called the *Mary Eliza* and the *Brother Jonathan*, a cattle scow, and two rowboats, as well as a 186-foot-long wharf. The ferry changed hands a few times over the following years. In 1872, a steamer named *Emily* was used to shuttle summer passengers between Shelter Island and Greenport. The ferry service continued to expand, and by 1930, carried over 143,000 passengers annually.

Pleasure boats have long been a part of the Greenport scene. In the late 1870s and early 1880s, the Atlantic Club started its regatta, or yacht cruise, at Greenport, with twenty-six boats, half of which belonged to the club. Around the same time, the New York Yacht Club had ten schooners and four sloops sailing from Glen Cove to Greenport (and from there to New London, Newport, and New Bedford) annually. In 1934, 200 pleasure craft (yachts, etc.) made Greenport their home, with another 250 entering the harbor seasonally.

The waterfront scenery has been an attraction for visitors since the early part of the nineteenth century. Before the arrival of the Long Island Rail Road in 1844, getting to Southold Town from points west required either a stagecoach or a boat, and much patience. Until the railroad came, mail to distant locales such as New York City was sent via packet ship. In 1844, the 96-mile railroad trip from Brooklyn to Greenport took three hours and thirty-five minutes. But even with the railroad's presence, Greenport remained quaint. An 1872 book called *Picturesque America* proclaimed: "Greenport is a very pretty town—as green, neat, and quiet, as the ideal New England village. The cottages that line the well-shaded streets are hid among trees, and nowhere is decay or unwholesome poverty apparent."

As of 1904, the hotels in Greenport included the Wyandank House, Booth House, Pipes Neck House, Stirlington House, Ye Clark House (established 1831), and the Commercial Hotel. The Booth House (on Sterling Avenue) was the largest of these, with accommodations for up to 125 people (though some accounts gave a higher number). Rates ranged from about $7 to $35 per week, with the hotel offering tennis, boating, bathing, and fishing. The *1921 Automobile Blue Book* had an advertisement for Steve's Vienna Restaurant and Hotel at 34 Front Street, which touted itself as "The most handsomely decorated and appointed Restaurant and Grill on east end of Long Island."

Greenport's reputation as a beach paradise grew during the mid-twentieth century as motels such as the Sound Shore (later Sound View) and Silver Sands opened west of downtown Greenport, catering to the automobile-driving tourists who could enjoy a full-on beach vacation experience while still being a stone's throw away from the historic village.

Of course, Greenport has changed over time, but the remaining vintage buildings of Main Street and Front Street, of which there are many, retain their authenticity and historic character, no matter what kind of shops have been installed within. From the earliest days, the commercial district of the village was centered around Main and Front Streets. Meanwhile, the residential section northwest of those streets is filled with nineteenth-century Victorian wonders that were originally built by the sea captains and merchants upon whose success the village was founded. The village docks, though now hosting magnificent yachts instead of schooners and clipper ships, have not lost their authenticity either. The marine tradition is still very much alive in Greenport, so it feels genuine and thriving, and not just like other places that are more of a nautical time capsule.

Over the years, Greenport has received many honors, ranging from being voted one of the prettiest towns in America to being named one of the fifty best yachting destinations in the country. This book offers some highlights from Greenport's long and storied history, from its early days as a whaling village through its colorful present as one of Long Island's most scenic and interesting locales. Within these pages you will find both the beauty of Greenport's recent days and intriguing mementos of the village of days past.

1

SEAPORT VILLAGE

Greenport has from the very start been a seaport village, with a heritage steeped in rich traditions of eastern Long Island and New England—from whaling to fishing to boating. Its authentic marine flavor permeates a downtown that is and always has been right on the waterfront, from its boat-lined wharves to nautical-themed restaurants such as the Frisky Oyster and Claudio's.

Southern view of Greenport, in Southold.

In 1844, the village of Greenport consisted of about 100 dwellings, three churches, a commercial district, and wharves. This period engraving of the village looks north up Main Street from the waterfront.

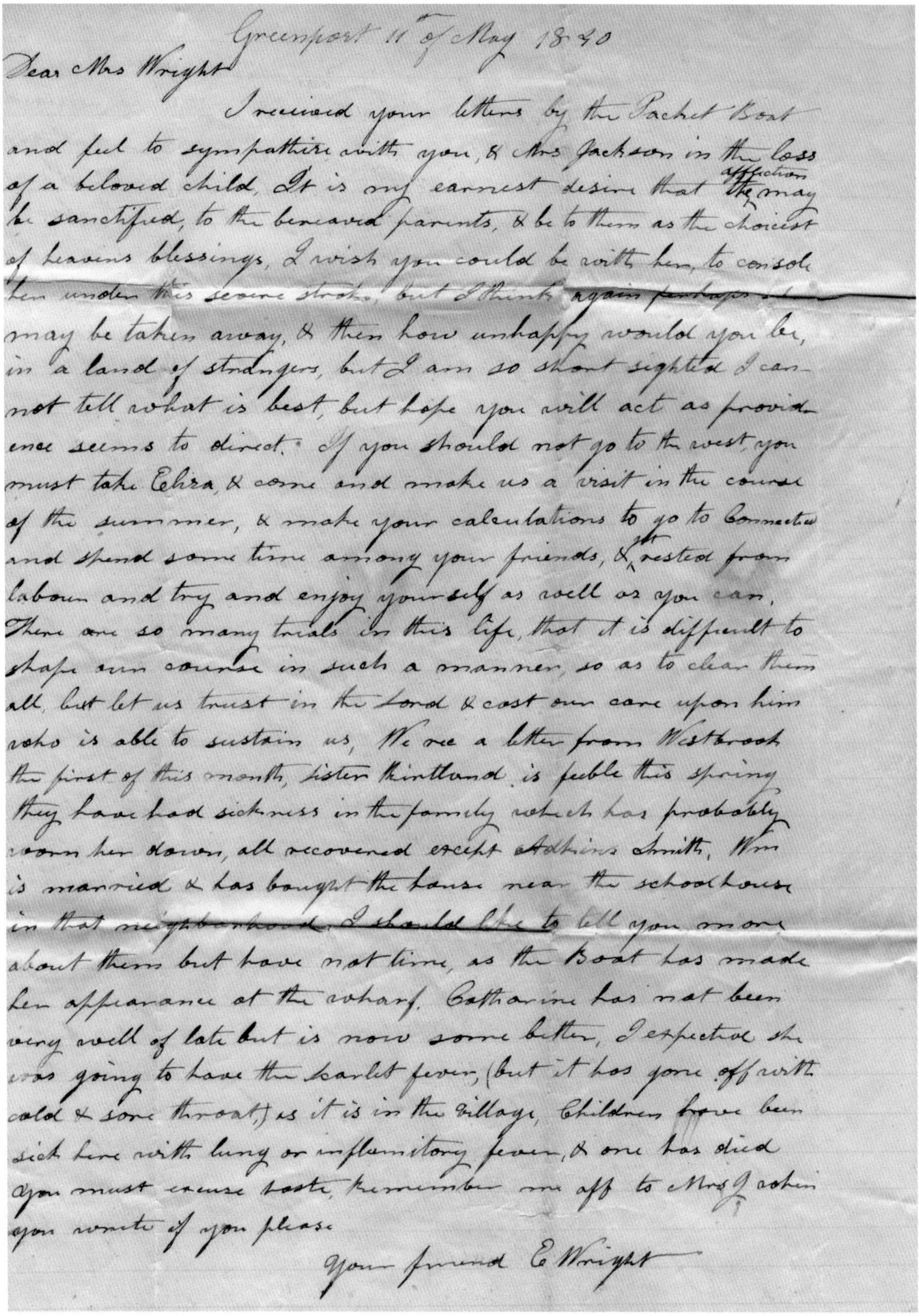

Greenport 11th of May 1840

Dear Mrs Wright

I recieved your letters by the Packet Boat and feel to sympathize with you, & Mrs Jackson in the loss of a beloved child, It is my earnest desire that affliction the may be sanctified, to the bereaved parents, & be to them as the choicest of heavens blessings, I wish you could be with her, to console her under this severe stroke, but I think again perhaps I may be taken away, & then how unhappy would you be, in a land of strangers, but I am so short sighted I cannot tell what is best, but hope you will act as providence seems to direct. If you should not go to the west, you must take Eliza, & come and make us a visit in the course of the summer, & make your calculations to go to Connecticut and spend some time among your friends, & rested from labour and try and enjoy yourself as well as you can, There are so many trials in this life, that it is difficult to shape our course in such a manner, so as to clear them all, but let us trust in the Lord & cast our care upon him who is able to sustain us, We rec a letter from Westbrook the first of this month, sister Kirtland is feeble this spring they have had sickness in the family which has probably worn her down, all recovered except Adkins Smith, Wm is married & has bought the house near the schoolhouse in that neighbourhood I should like to tell you more about them but have not time, as the Boat has made her appearance at the wharf, Catharine has not been very well of late but is now some better, I expected she was going to have the scarlet fever, (but it has gone off with cold & sore throat) as it is in the village, Children have been sick here with lung or inflamitory fever, & one has died You must excuse haste, Remember me aff to Mrs Jackson when you write if you please

Your friend E Wright

A letter sent from Greenport in 1840, during the height of the whaling days, is shown above; the text of the letter is reproduced on the following page. Early letters such as this one were often just folded sheets of paper that were addressed on the outside; in this case the letter was simply folded but sometimes the "envelope" was sealed with wax. *Note: Before the arrival of the railroad in Greenport in 1844, letters going to New York City were sent via packet boat.*

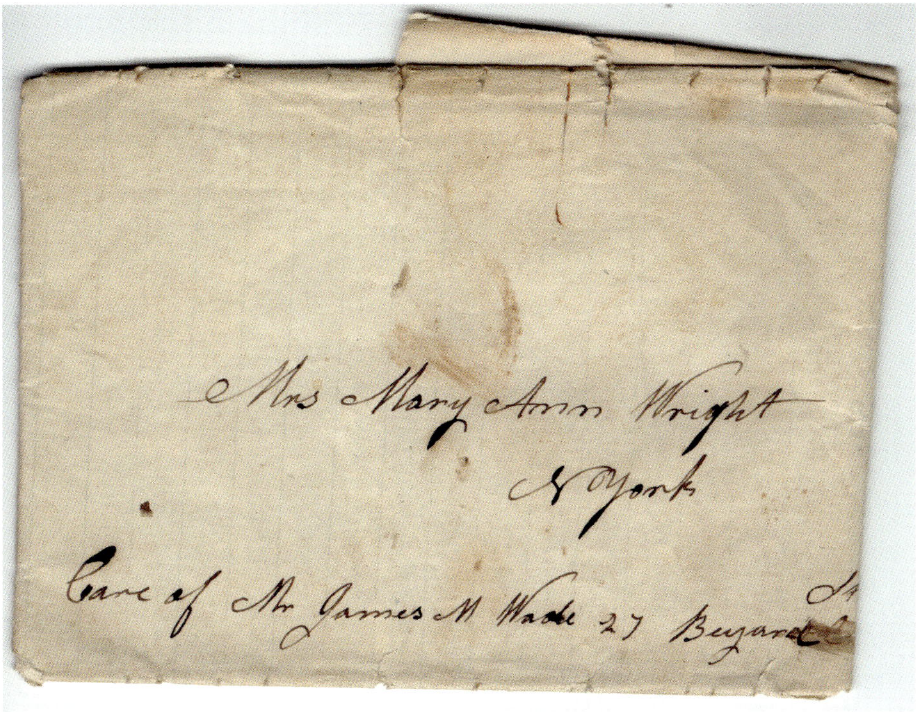

Greenport 11th May 1840 to Mrs. Mary Ann Wright in New York c/o Mr. James M. Wade, 27 Bayard Street

Dear Mrs. Wright,

I received your letter by the Packet Boat and feel to sympathize with you, & Mrs. Jackson in the loss of a beloved child. It is my earnest desire that the affection may be sanctified to the bereaved parents, & be to them as the choicest of heavens blessings, I wish you could be with her, to console her under this serene stroke, but I think again perhaps she may be taken away, & then how unhappy would you be in a land of strangers. But I am so short sighted I can not tell what is best, but hope you will act as providence seems to direct. If you should not go to the west, you must take Eliza & come and make us a visit in the course of the summer, & make your calculations to go to Connecticut and spend some time among your friends & rested from labor and try and enjoy yourself as well as you can. There are many trials in this life, that it is difficult to shape our course in such a manner so as to clear them all, but let us trust in the Lord & cast our care upon him who is able to sustain us. We owe a letter from Westbrook the first of this month, Sister Rintland is feeble this spring, they have had sickness in the family which has probably worn her down, all recovered except Adkins Smith. Wm is married & has bought the house near the schoolhouse in that neighborhood. I should be able to tell you more about this but have not time, as the Boat has made her appearance at the wharf. Catharine has not been very well of late but is now some better, I expected she was going to have the scarlet fever (but it has gone off with cold & sore throat) as it is in the village. Children here have been sick with lung or inflammatory fever & one has died. You must excuse haste, remember me off to Mrs. Jackson you write if you please.

Your friend E. Wright

This letter was sent from J. Cook of Greenport to Dr. Tredwell L. Ireland (1825-1913) of Miller Place on July 4, 1843. The letter was sealed on the back with red wax. It reads in part:

> You will doubtless be surprised to receive a letter from me, but I trust you will not think it intrusive at this time. I have heard that you are hoping that God in his rich grace has led you to become an heir of the inheritance purchased for us by Christ.
>
> In this I rejoice, and desire that you will be led by the same Spirit of Truth to "dig deep" and lay your foundation pure, upon the rock only, so that you shall never have reason to be ashamed of the hopes that you build upon it, but that they may stand amid the fearful glories of the great day of account.
>
> I have no doubt but that you have good instructors. I think it will be needless for me to remind you (at any length) that it was through Truth (Bible) that Christ prayed that his people might be sanctified; also, we are called into this vineyard to work. Now while you are yet young, I hope you will train yourself to habits of Christian enterprise and activity ... "

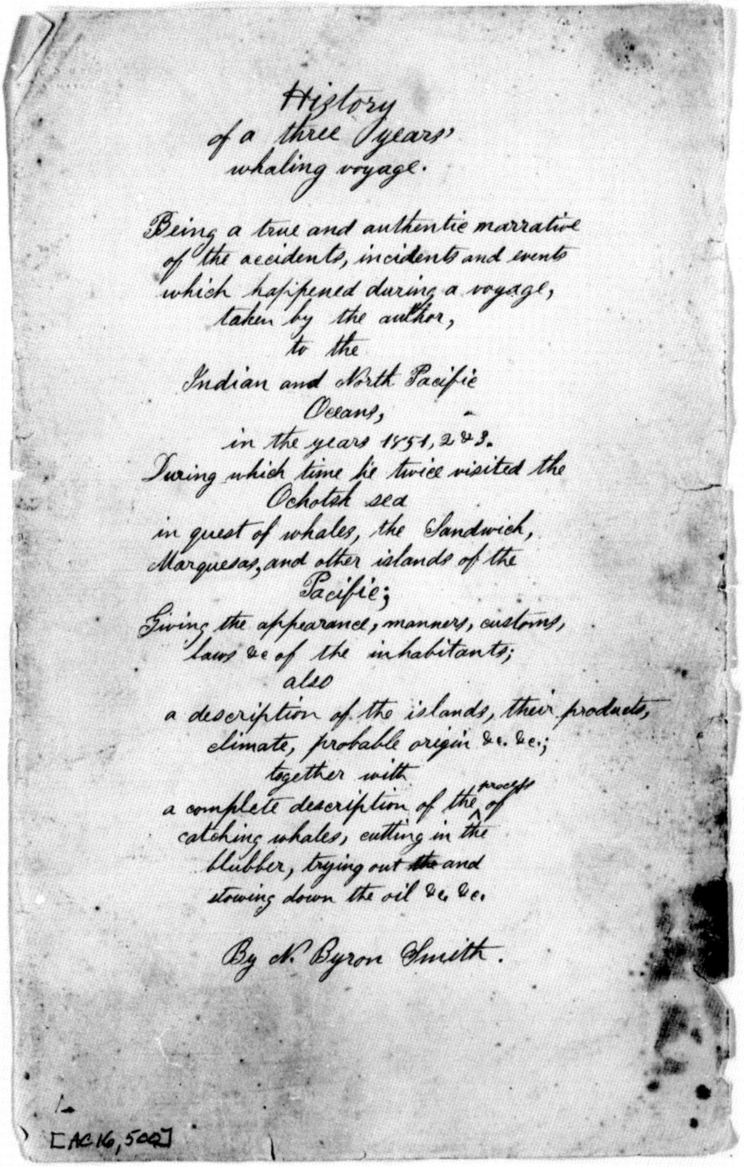

History
of a three years'
whaling voyage.

Being a true and authentic narrative
of the accidents, incidents and events
which happened during a voyage,
taken by the author,
to the
Indian and North Pacific
Oceans,
in the years 1851, 2 & 3.
During which time he twice visited the
Ochotsk sea
in quest of whales, the Sandwich,
Marquesas, and other islands of the
Pacific;
Giving the appearance, manners, customs,
laws &c of the inhabitants;
also
a description of the islands, their products,
climate, probable origin &c. &c.;
together with
a complete description of the process of
catching whales, cutting in the
blubber, trying out ~~the~~ and
stowing down the oil &c. &c.

By N. Byron Smith.

The cover page of a handwritten 148-page narrative by N. Byron Smith describing his experiences aboard the whaler *Nile of Greenport*, under the command of Captain Conklin, and his nearly three-year voyage (September 1851 to March 1854) to the whaling grounds in the Sea of Okhotsk in the northwest Pacific via the Azores, Cape of Good Hope, Indian Ocean, and New Zealand. In his story, Smith tells of capturing whales, extracting whale oil, life aboard the whaling ship, and his impressions of the people and culture of the Sandwich Islands and the Marquesas. Smith tells of first arriving in Greenport and preparing for the ocean voyage: "As may be supposed, our first desire on arriving at Greenport, was to behold the vessel in which we were now about to trust our lives and future hopes for a number of years, far out upon the stormy waves of the deep and dark blue ocean." Greenport was the last American settlement many whalers would see for years. In 1856, Greenport whaling ships brought in 675 barrels of sperm oil, 150 barrels of whale oil, and 4,000 pounds of whalebone.

An envelope sent from Greenport July 26, 1870, to Miss J. B. Moore of Greenport Village. On the back is a note about the departure of J. M. Corwin on that day at 6 am. Both Moore and Corwin were common surnames in the Town of Southold at the time.

First Train to Greenport in 1844

By CLARENCE ASHTON WOOD

A Glimpse of Greenport

From a Painting by Cyril A. Lewis, President of the Nassau County Art League

Published by the
LONG ISLAND FORUM
1944

PER COPY 50c

The cover and opening page of a 1944 booklet called "First Train to Greenport in 1844" celebrating the 100th anniversary of the arrival of the Long Island Rail Road in the village. The pamphlet includes the story of Preston Raynor, who in 1917 recounted his memories of that first train trip. "The first train was run over the tracks on July 27, 1844. Three trains were run carrying all passengers free," he wrote. "All engines burned wood, mostly pine ... At first the wood was thrown by hand into the engine tender but soon dump boxes were used dumping a load of wood into the tender at once ... Soon there was a train put on called the Boston Train, taking passengers and baggage to Greenport, then by steamer to Boston. Shortly the engines began setting the woods afire, killing some livestock ... Local people at one time became so enraged that they began tearing up sections of the track, causing several accidents."

Menhaden fishing and processing was big business in Greenport. According to an 1868 book: "Quite a fleet of schooners, sloops, and smacks may be seen in the harbor. There are even steam vessels of large size employed, which have machinery for extracting the oil on board ... There are seventeen oil factories in the vicinity of Greenport, but at a sufficient distance from town to prevent annoyance to the inhabitants." This print shows menhaden fishing on Long Island in 1884. At bottom, commercial fishing vessels at Greenport c1950s.

The 99-foot yacht Magnolia was built in 1883 and owned by Harry Belknap of Greenport. These days, magnificent yachts from far and wide dock in Greenport, some of which are worth tens of millions of dollars. At bottom, one of the most spectacular yachts ever built docked in Greenport in 2020. The Quantum of Solace, a 238-foot-long boat, was listed for $58 million. It has a crew of eighteen and can host fourteen guests in seven cabins.

This envelope postmarked 1886 from Portland, Maine, is addressed to Captain Truman Preston in Greenport. Preston had started S. T. Preston & Son Ship Chandlery at a prime location for serving sailors who docked in town—the end of Main Street, across from Claudio's. To this day, Preston's, one of the oldest surviving businesses on Long Island, offers a wide variety of marine-related items and is popular with boaters as well as tourists and visitors.

The cover of the "Of Ships & Sea" Preston's catalog from 1974. Besides offering marine supplies of all types, Preston's was known for selling ship models, marine pictures, and miscellaneous nautical keepsake items (and still to this day, but to a lesser extent now than in the past). The 1974 catalog was 142 pages and had dozens of photographs of everything from replica historical pistols to reproduction figureheads, to lamps, harpoons, belts, barometers, carved whales, and place mats. The catalog had seventy artworks, most of them framed color lithographs of ships of all kinds, and dozens of high-quality ship models (both finished hand-made ones and partly finished model kits).

An advertisement for Preston's *circa* 1980, and a 1970s image of the Preston's complex. The Ships and Sea Gallery space would later become a restaurant, which it still was as of 2021.

Claudio's Restaurant has been a Greenport waterfront legend since its founding in 1870 by Manuel Claudio. It was long the oldest same-family run restaurant in the country, until it was sold in 2018. The restaurant continues today under the same name. Upon its sale, the family put out a statement that read, in part: "While this marks the end of a long era for our family, we believe it also serves as a new beginning for the property, one which we hope will be filled with innovation and growth ... To our customers, we cannot thank you enough for your loyalty. Thank you for being the reason we got up every morning, thank you for all the good times you shared with us, thank you for making at least one visit to Claudio's every summer." At top, an image of the restaurant from the 1950s, and at bottom, in 2021.

The artist Edward Moran (1829-1901) was one of America's foremost maritime artists, and he set up a studio in Greenport with his sons, Percy and Leon. This envelope addressed from the First Bank of Greenport to Moran's Manhattan address in 1897 likely contained some business correspondence related to his artworks, perhaps a check (hence the "After 5 days, return to ... "). Moran's brother, Thomas, also a noted artist, later set up a studio on the South Fork. The undated sketch of Georgica Pond in East Hampton, shown here, was done by Edward.

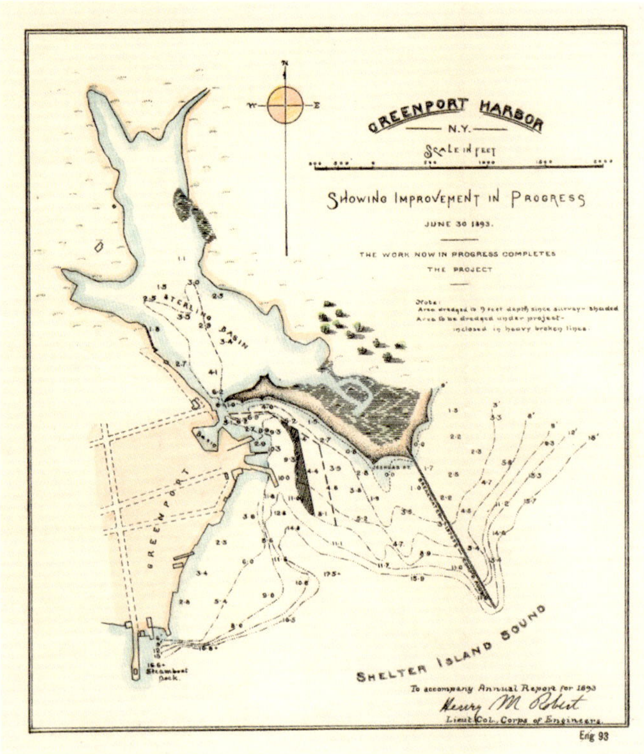

With time, and the disturbance of storms and constant ship traffic, silt can build up and make harbors shallower and therefore less suitable for docking. This 1893 map of Greenport harbor shows dredging work completed to that point in the shaded area—to a depth of nine feet. Also shown are areas that were still to be dredged "inclosed in heavy broken lines." Note some of the shallow depths on this map. At bottom, a 1949 map similarly notes water depths in Greenport.

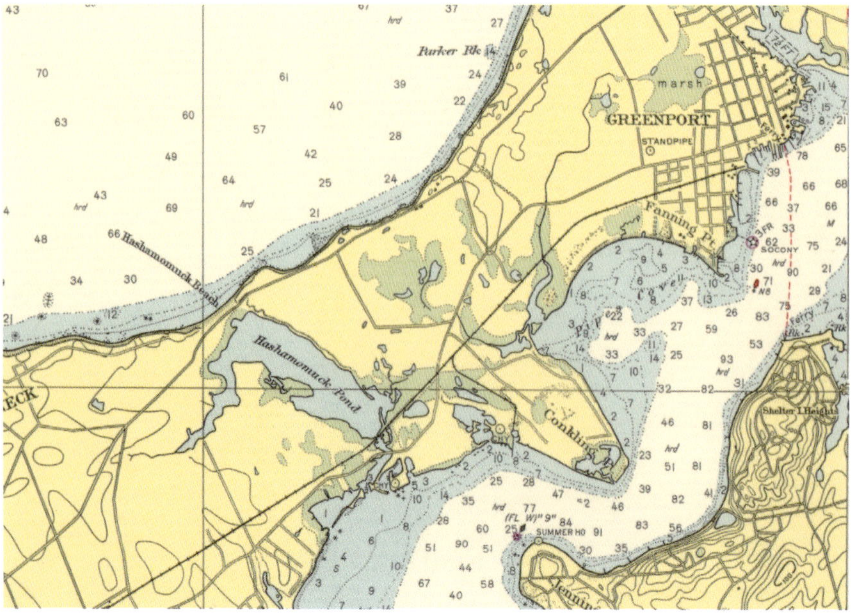

Greenport was very active in shipbuilding during World War I. At top, 72-foot-long submarine patrol boats were built for the Russian government c1917/18. At bottom, a February 1918 photo shows submarine chasers built for the U.S. Navy by the Greenport Construction Company. The boats had two 400 hp motors and could achieve a speed of 40 mph.

The *Chinagchgook* was built in 1916 by the Greenport Basin and Construction Co. It was named after a character from the book *Last of the Mohicans*. The photo shows the boat in Greenport. The boat was 60 feet long and had two 5-inch rapid fire guns. She was acquired by the Navy in May 1917, placed into service in June, but her gasoline tank exploded in July. She was beyond repair and thus destroyed in 1918.

A vintage ad for the Greenport Basin and Construction Company and the sign for the current iteration of the company. Boat construction and repairs is still an integral part of Greenport life to this day.

The locally famous Triangle Sea Sales opened in 1972 on Atlantic Avenue and relocated to its longtime location on South Street, diagonally across from the IGA Supermarket, in 1978. When the owners retired in 2018, the shop closed. At top, one corner inside the store photographed in 2017; at bottom, the exterior of the shop in 2016. The store offered all manner of nautical and marine-themed antiques and supplies, everything including oars, model ships, lanterns, shells, maps, prints, books, postcards, and ephemera. The store was soon after converted into Yard Sale Thrift Antiques.

Greenport has a connection to the famous America's Cup yacht races. Captain George Monsell, a lifelong Greenport resident, sailed three winning entries to victory—the *Enterprise* in 1930, the *Rainbow* in 1934, and the *Ranger* in 1937. At top is the *Enterprise*, and at bottom yachts docked in Greenport c1949.

A 1937 magazine advertisement for Elgin watches touts the fact that Greenport native Captain George Monsell brought an Elgin watch with him on the yacht the *Ranger*, which won the America's Cup race that year. The watches had a wide price range, from $18.50 all the way to $750.

The *Rachel and Ebenezer* was a schooner that was built in Maine in 1975 and for many years sailed out of Greenport as a coastal vacation sailing ship. At top is an advertisement from 1980 and at bottom a c1980s image of the boat docked in Greenport. As of 2017, the schooner was located in Florida and in bad need of repairs.

The steamer *Greenport*, seen in a photograph c1900, operated between New York City (near the foot of Wall Street) and Greenport, Shelter Island, Orient, Sag Harbor, and Block Island (Rhode Island). During summer months, it left New York at 5:30 pm every weekday and at 1 pm on Saturdays. At bottom, the Greenport-Shelter Island ferry in the 1950s. Much has changed over the last couple of centuries, but the need for ferries remains as there is no other way to travel from the North or South Forks to Shelter Island.

The ferry debarkation point Shelter Island in the 1950s and today. At the time of the top photo, the ferry slip was located at the foot of Main Street. The ferry between Shelter Island and Greenport is known as the North Ferry while the one traveling from Shelter Island to the South Fork is the South Ferry. The first scheduled ferry service from Greenport to Shelter Island began prior to 1850.

The Greenport to Shelter Island ferry as seen in the 1960s and in 2012. The ferry is currently operated by the North Ferry Co. and runs from 5 am to midnight every day, every ten to twenty minutes. As of 2022, the price of passage was $22 round trip for a vehicle and driver, with a $2 extra charge per additional person. The rate for foot passengers wanting to cross was $2 each way, and the price for bicyclists was $4 each way.

Greenport retains an authentic seaport flavor, from actual functional components such as a red light at the end of a dock in the village, to old mementos such as a vintage rusty anchor on the property of the Sound View Inn.

Boats docked in Greenport c1950s and in 2018. The deep-water harbor and relatively calm waters, thanks in part to the protection offered by Shelter Island, has made Greenport an ideal port for both commercial and pleasure craft through the decades.

Boats in the Stirling Basin c1950s and today. Though the docks just off Main Street and Front Street are more easily visible, there are dozens of boats that are docked in the basin.

The Long Beach Bar Light (aka Bug Light because of its appearance from a distance, looking like a bug walking on water) was originally built in 1870. It is technically located off of Orient, but it is easily visible from eastern Greenport as it lies less than three miles due east; the Normal E. Klipp Marine Park is a good viewing point. It was first built as a screwpile lighthouse. A reinforced concrete foundation was added in 1926. The current building is a 1990 replica of the older one, which was burned by arsonists in 1963. Above, the lighthouse on a vintage postcard, and inset, as seen from Norman E. Klipp Marine Park in 2021.

Originally built as the *Ranger* in 1876, the gunboat at top was renamed the *Nantucket* in 1918 and was used during World War I. The ship was later turned into a training ship, shown here c1940 in Greenport (she was scrapped in 1958). But tall ships are not just a thing of the past in Greenport, they can still be seen to this day, and not just during the annual Maritime Festival. At bottom, a tall ship docked in Greenport in 2012. In 2015, Tall Ships America declared Greenport the Tall Ships Port of the Year.

2

Around Town

Greenport Village is an eclectic, exciting place whose shops and restaurants cater to a variety of people including its own residents, vacationers, day trippers, and mariners. The commercial heart of the village, Main and Front Streets, has changed a great deal over the years, and yet in many ways has retained its nineteenth-century vibe. Though Greenport has grown, it has not overgrown, and remains a true gem of the North Fork.

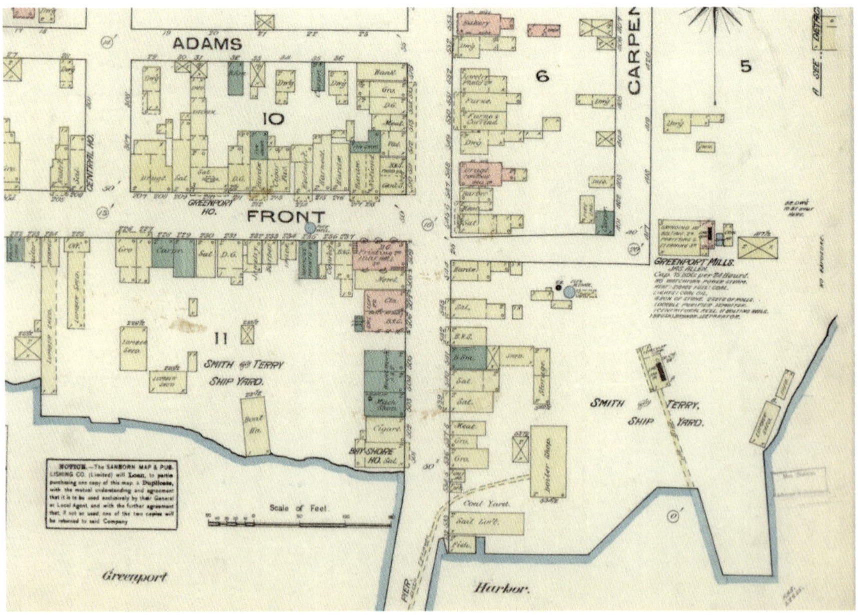

The Sanborn Fire Insurance Company created detailed maps of Greenport in the late nineteenth and early twentieth centuries. This image shows the 1885 version of the map. Fire was a much more serious risk in the days of old, as more buildings were made of wood and there were generally more fire hazards around—everything from kerosene and coal to fireplaces. These maps offered detailed information about the exact type, size, and location of Greenport's buildings.

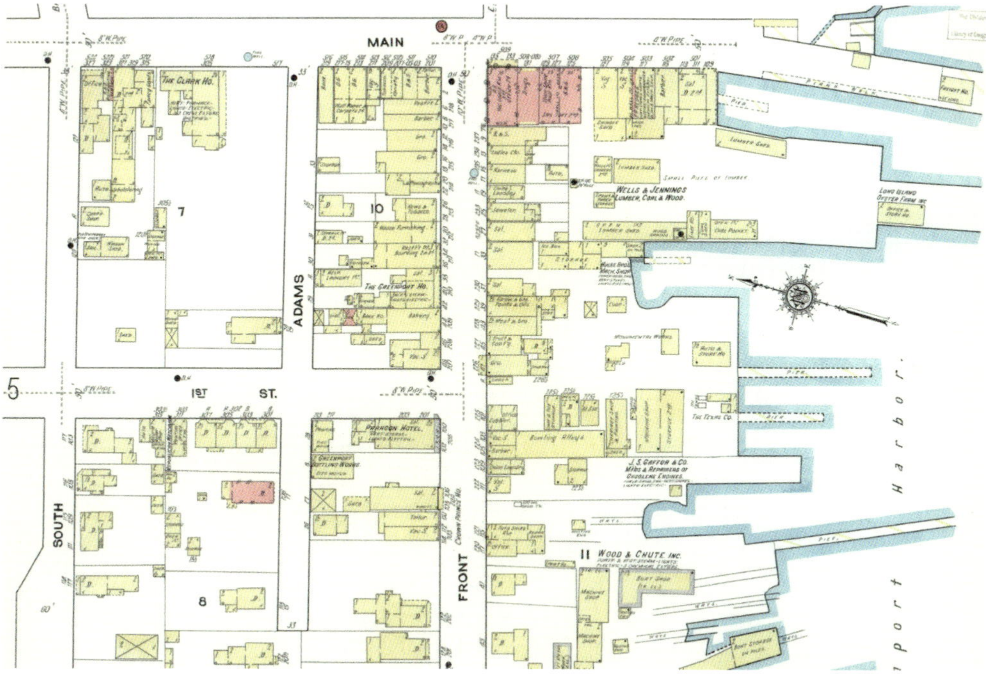

A pair of Sanborn maps from 1917 shows the continued development of the village. At top, three hotels are visible in this image: the Clark House, Greenport Hotel, and Paragon Hotel. At bottom, the industrial nature of the businesses on the east side of Main Street is evident: auto repairs, ship yards, tin smith, electrical contractor, etc.

New York's Lieutenant Governor Lewis Stuyvesant Chanler visited Greenport in 1908 while campaigning for governor. He lost the race to Republican Charles Evans Hughes, 804,651 to 735,189. These two images show Chanler walking the streets of Greenport in October 1908.

A 2020 historic resources survey of Greenport's buildings detailed the wide variety of period architectural gems in the village, including homes, commercial buildings, and churches built in the Federal, Greek Revival, Gothic Revival, Italianate, Queen Anne, and Colonial Revival styles from the late eighteenth to early twentieth centuries. At bottom is an Italianate style home just off Main Street photographed in 2015, and at top ornate details of the late nineteenth century Reeve's Building on Main Street, photographed in 2012. In the early days of the building, the Freemasons met on the second floor.

At top, the old wood frame Greenport Municipal Building seen c1940, and at bottom, the attractive present-day Village Hall at the intersection of 3rd and South streets, two blocks north of Front Street.

The section of Front Street adjacent to Main Street is actually more attractive today than it was in the vintage image at top, c1940s. The electrical poles are now gone, and some trees line the street.

The Arcade was since 1928 a fixture in the heart of Greenport Village. A department store in the small-town tradition, it carried all manner of things—from clothing to greeting cards to toys. In its final years, under a new owner since 2012, it was in decline compared to prior boom years, until it closed in 2017. At top, the inside of the store in 2016, at bottom the empty (though actually still filled with merchandise) store in 2021.

Restaurants come and go in Greenport as everywhere. Some stay a long time, such as The Coronet Luncheonette, which graced the high visibility corner of Main and Front Streets for many years, an iconic eatery that seemed happily stuck in the 1950s. The restaurant closed its doors in 2016, and soon after reopened as Crazy Beans, a restaurant that remained in many ways faithful to the feel of the original place. Top inset, the legendary sign as photographed in 2013.

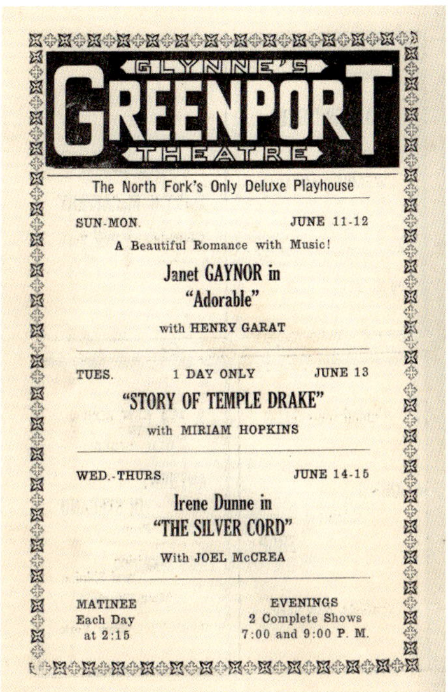

GLYNNE'S
GREENPORT
THEATRE

The North Fork's Only Deluxe Playhouse

SUN-MON. JUNE 11-12

A Beautiful Romance with Music!

Janet GAYNOR in
"Adorable"
with HENRY GARAT

TUES. 1 DAY ONLY JUNE 13

"STORY OF TEMPLE DRAKE"
with MIRIAM HOPKINS

WED.-THURS. JUNE 14-15

Irene Dunne in
"THE SILVER CORD"
With JOEL McCREA

MATINEE
Each Day
at 2:15

EVENINGS
2 Complete Shows
7:00 and 9:00 P. M.

A 1933 advertisement for Glynne's Greenport Theatre on Front Street, built as the Metro Theatre. It was bought by Long Island theater investor Mike Glynne in 1930. The building was destroyed by the hurricane of 1938 and was replaced with the current theater building.

Main Street block of buildings c1950 and in 2021. Note the building on the corner in the vintage image features a sign pointing toward Claudio's. This particular section of Main Street has changed considerably; only two of the buildings in the vintage image still stand today.

Greenport has long been known for its interesting variety of shops and boutiques. Nautical themed ones such as Sea Bags (a New England chain store whose Greenport location opened in 2016) are especially fitting for this nineteenth-century seaport. Goldin Furniture occupies a historic nineteenth-century building on Main Street; many Greenport shops are housed in beautiful Victorian structures.

During the Covid-19 pandemic, Greenport, like all vacation getaway destinations, tried to make the best of a difficult situation. A sign in August 2020 touts masks for sale, while another reminds patrons to wear masks.

Over the years, Greenport has had dozens of antique shops. Some have lasted for decades while others have come and gone. Above, the ever-popular Lydia's Antiques and Stained Glass in 2021 and inset a vintage "Piggy Cook" for sale in a village antique shop in 2013. There is always an interesting variety of vintage items on display at any given time.

The Rhumb Line Bar and Restaurant on Front Street (ad above c1981) was a Greenport fixture, the long-time neighbor of the Whiskey Wind Tavern. The Rhumb Line closed in 2016 and Andy's Restaurant opened in its place in 2017. Bottom: For many years, the selection of miniature plastic ducks at Goldsmith's toy store has been a top attraction for kids of all ages, with new ones being introduced regularly. These novelty ducks have often graced the front window of the store; this is a display from 2011.

Many Greenport businesses have lasted several decades. After twenty-five years in business, the beloved candy and gift shop Sweet Indulgences went out of business in 2021 when its owner retired and the building was sold. Seen at top in 2015 and at bottom not long before its closing in the fall of 2021.

The North Fork Trading Post antique store on Route 25 offered an interesting array of vintage items. At top, the store in 2017 and at bottom during a 2021 tag sale after its closure. The owner, Robert Adipietro, had died in 2020. Numerous wares were usually in front of the store to attract passersby.

Greenport is full of interesting little vintage details that deserve a moment or two to observe. At top, an old ship's wheel and at bottom a ship painted on the side exterior wall of Preston's.

The beautiful and historic Carousel is one of the focal points of the village, playing host to countless thousands of children every year. Built in 1920, the wooden carousel was originally part of a traveling carnival. In 1955, it wound up at the Grumman plant in Calverton. The Village of Greenport acquired it in 1997 and was moved to the newly opened Mitchell Park in 2001. At top, a closeup of a carousel horse in 2012. At bottom the Carousel in 2021.

Mitchell Park gave Greenport exactly what it needed as a historic and scenic seaport village—a public park and space that is in the heart of downtown and is a minute's walk to shops and restaurants, has plenty of seating and open space for various events and gatherings, and also offers unmatched views of the waterfront. At top, a vintage car meet in the park in 2010, and at bottom, a display of vintage local fire engines in Mitchell Park in the summer of 2018 and a concert in progress in the park in the summer of 2021. It seems like there's always something interesting happening at the park. In recent years, the Monday Night Dancing in the Park features live music and dancing on summer nights, from country to reggae to rock to salsa and more.

Reeve Park (aka Reeve's Park) is located at the confluence of First and Main Streets. The top image c1910 predates the World War I, World War II, and Korean/Vietnam monuments that were added over the years.

Greenport's railroad station location makes it more easily accessible to downtown than many Long Island stations. It is also just a stone's throw from the ferry to Shelter Island and is adjacent to the Railroad Museum of Long Island and the East End Seaport Museum. At top, the station c1910s and at bottom in 2021.

A 1933 ad for Meadowbrook Farm Dairy. Inset, a milk bottle cap from Fair View Farm.

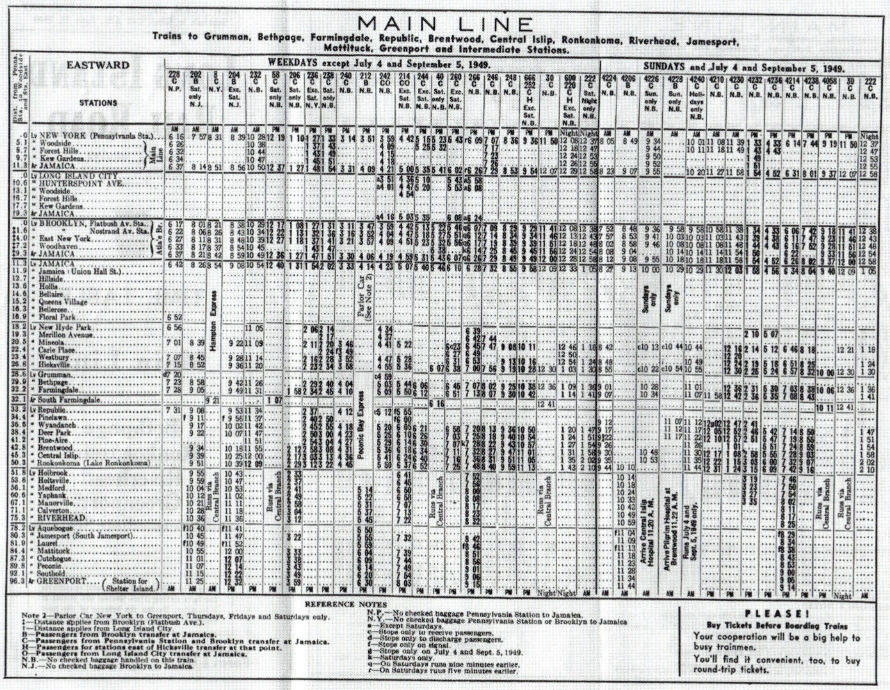

A Long Island Rail Road “Main Line” train schedule from May 1949 shows Greenport as the last stop (which it still is). An evening trip from Greenport to Jamaica took two hours and eighteen minutes in 1949; in 2021, the same trip took two hours twenty-seven minutes.

Greenport has a vibrant and colorful nightlife, whether it's the lively restaurants and shops on Front and Main Streets, or one of the Claudio's waterfront eateries, where the lights from boats and docks light the dark evening sky and reflect in the water.

Though many East End settlements were founded in the seventeenth century, it was not until the nineteenth century that the Catholic Church began to organize on Long Island. This was simply because it was not until the 1830s that Catholic immigrants of any number began to arrive in New York. The first Catholic Church building in Greenport was erected around 1855, but there was no organized parish. The present church, St. Agnes, was built in 1884 and dedicated by Bishop John Loughlin.

The Methodist Episcopal Church, on Main Street, seen at top c1905, was built in 1880. The building was sold by the United Methodist Church in 2017 for an estimated $950,000. It was soon after converted to a rental property that could accommodate up to sixteen guests in six bedrooms.

The Gothic Revival style "Old Church" (1879) on Fifth Avenue is a handsome former Lutheran church that is now a private residence. The congregation outgrew the church and in the mid-1960s a new one was built west of the village. A humorous sign lies in front.

At top is the 1879 Greenport high school building, which did not have indoor bathrooms until 1895. By the turn of the twentieth century, the building was already too small (and did not have a gymnasium); in 1901 (around when this photo was taken) there were already over 600 students crammed into the building. The new, much larger Art Deco style school opened in 1933, at bottom seen in 2018 and inset c1950s.

An earlier version of the Greenport post office c1960s which stood next to Colonial Drugs, and the present-day post office on the south side of Front Street.

The Eastern Long Island Hospital c1960s and today as the Stony Brook Eastern Long Island Hospital, located on Manor Place. The hospital began its operations c1905 in a mansion donated by its owners, the Wood sisters. As of 2020, the hospital had seventy beds and that year fielded 6,112 ER visits and 23,262 outpatient visits, and employed 338 people.

The old Greenport Opera House Building was built in 1899 as a replacement for Stirling Hall, a structure that had burnt down. Famous actor William Gillette was among those who performed at the Opera House. After its time as a performance space was over, it had some commercial uses before it was demolished in 1956. At top, the building as seen c1905. At bottom, the site is now occupied by a bank parking lot.

Greenport has a history of beverage production going back into the nineteenth century. The Stirling Bottling Works (aka Sterling) on Main Street was in operation from the late nineteenth century through well into the twentieth century. For a time, it co-existed with the Greenport Bottling Works on Front Street. In 2009, the Greenport Harbor Brewing Company opened in an old firehouse on Carpenter Street, offering a wide variety of beers including limited releases such as Chocolate Covered Cherry Pie and Double Duck Porter.

3

BEACHES, VACATIONS, AND CELEBRATIONS

With its scenic waterfront setting, Greenport has from the beginning been an attractive place to visit. An 1845 book said of Greenport: "Its bright verdure, and the grace of its waving acacia shades, render the drives in its vicinity very agreeable to the lover of fine scenery." The nature of a "vacation" in Greenport has changed with the growing popularity of the automobile and the opening of motels west of town in the mid-twentieth century, and Greenport is more popular than ever.

The first mention of Greenport hospitality dates to 1757, when it is said that a young George Washington visited "Booth House" while awaiting a ferry to Connecticut. At that time, there were only a few buildings in Greenport. The later Booth House Hotel at Sterling Creek was a large building facing the Sterling Basin, accommodating over 100 guests. The Booth House Hotel shown in this image was very popular in the late nineteenth and early twentieth centuries. It burned down in the 1960s.

The Clarke House (aka Clark) was established in 1831 and originally catered to sea captains and whalers who were in Greenport before their voyage set sail. In its nearly century-long tenure, the inn welcomed such notables as John Quincy Adams and General Winfield Scott. Today the site is occupied by the historic c1750s Ireland House, which was originally 100 feet from its current location.

The Townsend Manor Inn on Main Street (c1950s view above) is housed in a historic building that dates back to 1835, when a whaling captain named Cogswell built the large home. It was first opened as an inn in 1926, when Lillian Cook Townsend debuted Ye Olde Townsend Inn. Because of the shape of Stirling Basin, the historic inn's property actually fronts the water. Inset: A 1930 advertisement for the inn.

67 Steps Beach on the Sound shore of Greenport, just off the North Road, offers spectacular views of the rocky coastline and sometimes rough seas. The beach is named for the exact number of steps it takes to get down to the sand. At top, seen in a vintage view from c1940s and at bottom in a present-day view. In 2018, volunteers cleaned up 1,100 pounds of debris from the beach.

Shelter Island, just a short ferry ride away from Greenport, has numerous vantage points in the Dering Harbor and Shelter Island Heights communities that offer great views of Greenport view. At top, the massive 700-foot-long Manhansett Hotel, c1904, which stood at Dering Harbor just east of Locust Point and at bottom, the sunset and Greenport as seen from the hotel property c1905.

At top, a c1950s view from Jenning's Point on Shelter Island, looking toward Greenport. At bottom, the view toward Greenport from the Pridwin Hotel property on Shelter Island in 2008.

A postcard showing Bay Avenue written c1917 or 1918. The note says: "Am having a lovely visit with Jane with some good times thrown in—was out black berrying this AM, in torpedo boat yesterday & in launch in the PM. Milton is thriving on the salt air. Wish you could be here with me." At bottom, present-day Bay Avenue.

The relatively calm waters of the Peconic offer Greenport beachgoers a pleasant experience. At top, a waterfront scene in 1905 and at bottom, the view from the Silver Sands beach in 2017.

Sterling Street as seen c1910 and present-day. One of Greenport's most scenic roads, Sterling starts at Main Street just south of the Townsend Manor Inn, heads toward Stirling Basin, hugs the shoreline and then goes west until it dead ends at Carpenter Street.

The exterior of the Sound Shore Motel *circa* the 1960s. The motel was built in 1953 as a twelve-unit motel by Jack and Donna Levin (Jack Levin died in 2012 at the age of 105). It was added to over the years. At bottom, the exterior of the Sound View Motel in 2004.

Room 22 at the Silver Sands Motel faces the water. Seen here at top in a c1970s image, the room's decor is typical for both the rooms and the cottages, which all have a genuine vintage feel. Numerous film and magazine shoots have taken place at the motel over the years. At bottom, the iconic vintage Silver Sands sign on a summer 2010 night.

The Silver Sands Motel, with its authentic vintage feel, has been the setting for numerous video shoots, magazine shoots, and even a feature film. The political thriller *18½*, set in Nixon-era 1974, directed by Dan Mirvish and starring Bruce Campbell, John Magaro, Richard Kind, Willa Fitzgerald, Vondie Curtis-Hall, Jon Cryer, Catharine Curtin, and Ted Raimi, was filmed at the motel in 2020. The motel's own Terry Keefe was a co-producer of the film.

John Magaro (Paul) and Willa Fitzgerald (Connie) star in Dan Mirvish's film "18½"
photo credit: Elle Schneider ©2021, Waterbug Eater Films, LLC

Located on Route 25 west of Greenport Village, the Drossos Motel and Snack Bar was built by Alexandra and John Drossos and dates to the 1950s. It is known for its snack stand and miniature golf course.

Two c1960s interior views of Mitchell's Restaurant, one showing the attractive bar and the other showing the dining room. This popular waterfront eatery (with its own marina) was located on the site of present-day Mitchell Park. A longtime Greenport favorite, it burned down in 1978 and was eventually replaced with the present-day park and carousel.

At top, an advertisement for the Sterlington Hotel from 1981. The building, located on Third Street, was constructed in the 1840s and named the Sterlington Hotel in 1894. It became a restaurant in 1980, but by 2016, it was falling apart. A new owner purchased it and restored the building, which as of 2022 housed Goldberg's Famous Bagels and apartments.

This elegant Victorian building on the North Road has a long history as a restaurant. It was for a long time Porky's, as seen in this c1960s image at top. Later, it became the Shady Lady (opened 2002), and then the Lin Beach House (opened 2018), a six-room hotel with a bar downstairs.

The Island's End Golf and Country Country Club (opened in 1962) as seen in 1964 and at bottom in 2021. The back of the vintage postcard says: "The golf course covers our farm and two adjacent ones. Can barely see the barn. Magnifying glass will help." There are 40,000 trees on the course.

Every East End village has a few landmark businesses that everyone seems to know, and Claudio's is one of Greenport's most well-known. This vintage 1981 advertisement makes it evident that for many arriving by water, Claudio's was the first and most prominent sight to greet them.

Greenport is a village for all seasons. At top, autumn decorations in front of Lucharito's in October 2021, and at bottom, dozens of American flags fly proudly in Mitchell Park on Veterans Day 2021.

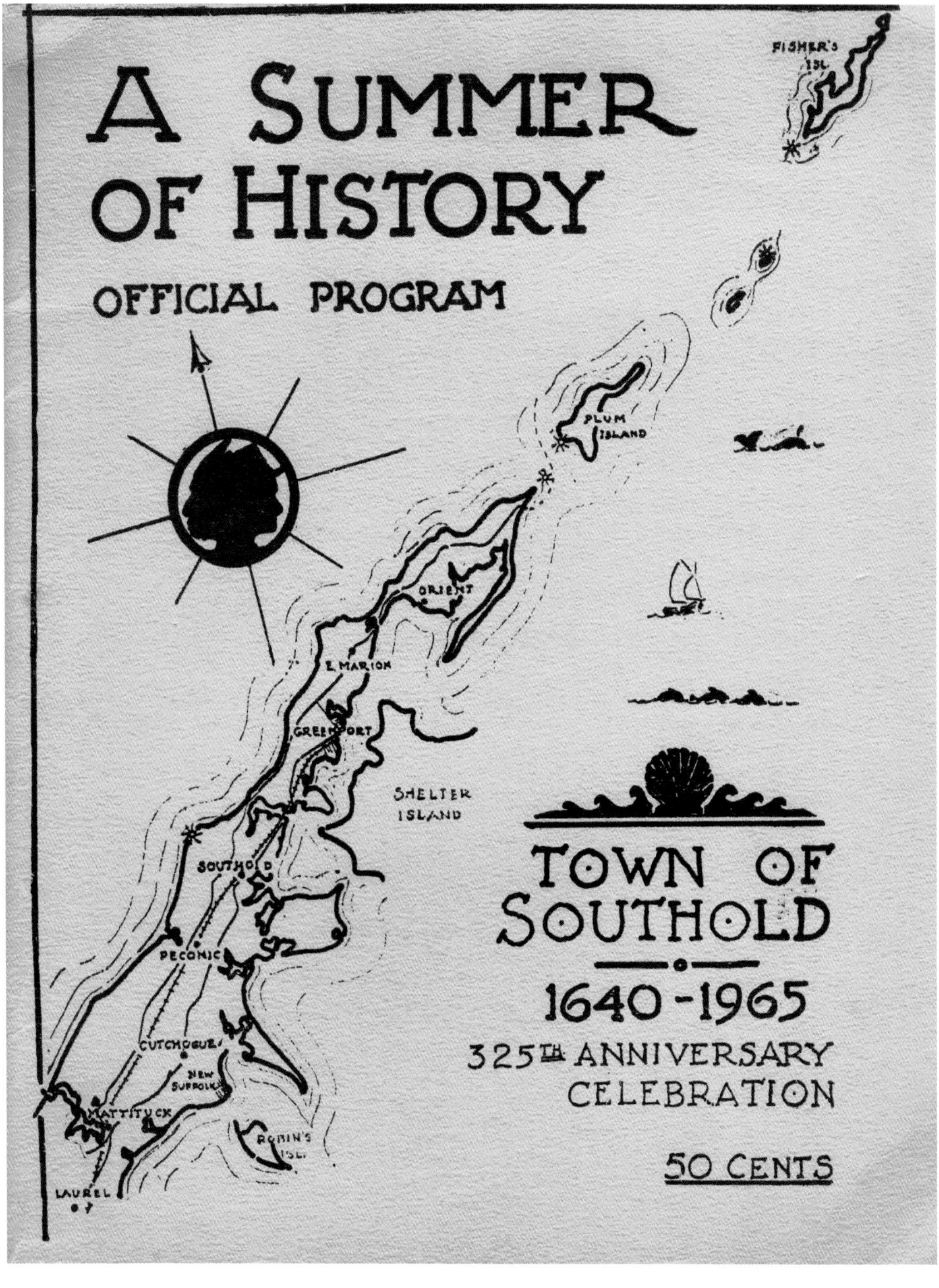

The cover of the Town of Southold's 325th Anniversary program. Inside was a letter from Town Supervisor Lester Albertson, proclaiming, "Southold is an important part of the fastest growing county in the country and is experiencing steady growth." The booklet contains a list of local events that celebratory summer, including several in Greenport, such as the Grand Boat Parade from Greenport Harbor to Founders' Landing in Southold, a naval vessel on display in Greenport Harbor, and the Greenport Fire Department's Annual Block Party.

The colorful lights emanating from the boats docked in Greenport offer shimmering nighttime views of the waterfront.

4

NATURE

There's so much to see and do in and around Greenport that it's easy to get caught up in all the shopping, eating, and boating that the village has to offer. But nature calls, literally, and a closer look at some of the area's flora and fauna can be very rewarding. From fish to crabs to birds to deer, animal life is plentiful in Greenport, as is the area's wide variety of marine plants, trees, and wildflowers.

If you step into the water at one of Greenport's beaches, chances are you'll run into some fish, like these spotted in 2015.

At top, an aerial view looking north from Shelter Island toward Greenport in 1930 from an altitude of 3,500 feet, and at bottom, a c1960s aerial view of Greenport taken from west of downtown.

Greenport wetlands such as these at Pipes Cove attract a variety of marine species, including egrets. At top, a ground-level view of the Pipes Cove wetlands in 2018, and at bottom, an aerial view in 2021.

Greenport offers two very different experiences of the waterfront—the rocky and rougher seas of the Sound shore to the north and the calmer waters of the Peconic Bay to the south. The protected waters of Greenport village's harbor have always been the place where ships and boats of all sizes have anchored, rather than the seas of the Sound shore. At top, a view of the Sound shore *circa* 1950, and at bottom in 2012.

Ospreys are large raptors that can live up to thirty years. Once considered endangered in New York State, they have made a comeback along the coastline and there are several that nest in Greenport. These ospreys were photographed in their nest atop a pole near the Silver Sands Motel, at top in 2011 and bottom 2021.

A sandpiper looking for food on a Greenport beach in 2008 (top) and a seagull perched on a post in 2015 (bottom). Pay close attention and you'll notice just how many different kinds of bird species make Greenport their home. From 1979 to 2018, the very popular Sandpiper Ice Cream Shop was located on Main Street, which then became the Greenport Creamery in 2019.

Greenport offers some fun sights for rock hobbyists. At top, a Greenport boulder contains pinkish-red crystals. At bottom, some of the countless smooth wave-washed pebbles that can be found on Greenport beaches.

A great variety of shellfish can be found in Greenport's waters, including clams, oysters, conch, drills, tellins, and scallops. Above, a conch shell photographed in 2013, and at right, a scallop shell found in 2017.

Besides the sea, Greenport offers other ways to experience nature. Above, a scene in the Arshamomaque Preserve off Chapel Lane in 2021.

At top, a Monarch butterfly spotted in 2010 on a sunflower. At bottom, a deer seen in Greenport West in 2015. Deer are definitely a presence in the area (as is the case in much of Suffolk County, for better or worse).

The marine environment of Greenport plays host to numerous species of flowering plants and shrubs that thrive in sandy soil close to the water.

There are few places on Long Island where sunsets can match the beauty that can be found in Greenport. At top a view of a Greenport sunset in 1962, and at bottom, a sunset in 2015 from the Sound View Restaurant.

At top, sunset in the village in 2017, and at bottom, a bright moon reflects on the water on an August night in 2021.

AFTERWORD

Reflections on Filming at a Legendary Greenport Location

By Richard Kind

Richard Kind plays the Silver Sands Motel manager in the independent film *18½*, which was shot on location at the Silver Sands Motel in Greenport in 2020. In addition, he has appeared in dozens of television shows and films over the last thirty-five years, including *Mad About You*, *Spin City*, *Curb Your Enthusiasm*, *Inside Out*, and *A Serious Man*.

When I arrived at the Silver Sands Hotel, or I suppose it's a motel, it seemed unappealing. throwback of style so old fashioned as to perhaps be uncomfortable. I was wrong. It is a gem. They have kept it pristine, inviting, and rather than modernize a beautiful location, they have worked hard to maintain its charm. looked more like an old Jersey Shore motel rather than a Hamptons-esque facility. Of course, the view and location are beyond compare.

I live in a classic Upper West Side apartment and my wooden hallway floors have a subtle but definite slant. If you place a ball at the top, it will roll down. Years of buckling and wear have created this unevenness. When I bought the unit, I thought this was charming. If I sell the place, someone may totally level the floor and replace it with different wood or tile. That would be a person whose tastes are different than mine.

Such a place is the Silver Sands.

Is the grass in the courtyard pristine? No. It's near the salt water.

Are the rooms glamorous? No. They are charming and have retained every bit of their mid-century charm.

Could it be fixed up and modernized? I suppose so. But why? It would be just another hotel. The sign out front, the roadside shape of the compound, the tchotchkes in the entry and at the front desk, where I shot all my scenes, took years and years to weather and look like that. Such character doesn't just appear overnight.

I was lucky enough to talk with the owners, and they talked about selling. They live in a small unit adjoining the front entry. And for a second, I dreamt of being a proprietor of a hotel that I purchased. That charming spot. And they could get a lot of money, because you knock down the hotel and you've got some mighty prime real estate. I hope that never happens. This gem should be maintained. Worked on to maintain what once was. I don't know who their clientele is. I don't know how much they charge for a room. I have no idea how they fared through two seasons of Covid. But if you're lucky enough to escape this divisive, internet-driven world and step back into a bucolic seaside edifice with no pretensions of modernization much less entry into the twenty-first century, you could not find a better place than the Silver Sands.